C.H.SISSON

Selected Poems

FOREWORD BY M. L. ROSENTHAL

A NEW DIRECTIONS BOOK

Published by arrangement with Carcanet Press Limited, Manchester.

Manufactured in the United States of America.
New Directions Books are printed on acid-free paper.
First published as New Directions Paperbook 826 in 1996.
Published simultaneously in Canada by Penguin Books Canada Limited.

Library of Congress Cataloging-in-Publication Data
Sisson, C. H. (Charles Hubert), 1914–
    Selected poems / C. H. Sisson ; with a foreword by M. L. Rosenthal.
      p.   cm.
    ISBN 0–8112–1327–7 (acid-free paper)
    I.   Title.
    PR6037.I78A6
    821'.914—dc20   95–47599
                                                                      CIP

Celebrating 60 years of publishing for James Laughlin
by New Directions Publishing Corporation
80 Eighth Avenue, New York 10011

Contents

Foreword by M. L. Rosenthal

Foreword

"Poets," said Robert Frost, "have always been beggars." That's not just a matter of money, but also of getting their work printed. The present volume, for instance, is C. H. Sisson's first to find an American publisher in many years.

A rational explanation for this neglect would be hard to ferret out. It cannot be the depressive life-vision—one widely shared in our time—of this established British poet now in his eighties. Anyway, his wry wit and sudden tonal leaps liven up the gloom considerably. An apt example is "The Nature of Man," which begins as a moment of thoughtful speculation, turns quickly into a harsh caricature of ordinary city folk as "ape-like" automatons wearing human masks, and at last dives surrealistically into the dream-life, seeing us all as "plants or undiscovered worlds."

Nor is Sisson's death-obsession likely to shock American readers even when, in "Moriturus," the author calls himself (and everyone else) a "carcase that awaits the undertaker." This, after all, is the century of grim elegists in every country, among them the war and Holocaust poets. Sisson's affinity with their spirit is seen, typically, in his remorse-driven little elegy "Somerton Moor," a richly compressed parallel to Hardy's "Poems of 1912–13."

Nor, again, does his kinship with other figures of this century emerge only in the realms of elegy and despair. Among many diverse instances, his "Virgini Senescens" and "The Regrets" both resemble Yeats's "The Wild Old Wicked Man" in contrasting virtuous maidenhood and lustful old age. A poem like "The Hare" is tonally close to Edward Thomas and Robert Frost; and more surprisingly, the early "On a Troopship" could almost be one of Charles Olson's *Maximus Poems*. Certain serious pieces of some length, such as "In Insula Avalonia" and "Trivia," may remind us of Laura Riding's struggles to render elusive metaphysical and self-analytical insights lyrically. And little poems like "A Duckling" and "In Time of Famine: Bengal" are as tenderly, if unsentimentally, humane as anything by Dilys Laing or James Wright.

For most contemporary readers, the alien side of Sisson is his extreme religious humility, with Tory overtones (like those of Ford Madox Ford) unfamiliar on this side of the Atlantic. Its austerity forbids confident assertions about faith in divinity or in meaning or even in the reality of one's own life. And when ardently Christian and pastoral notes do appear along the way, they are most often rooted in a mystically conservative English localism.

In "The Hare," Sisson recalls a conversation with a local farmer on a field the poet once owned. The two of them, he says, were mere "denizens" of the land, "trenched in antiquity," around them. He dreams of total absorption in the elemental, essential England antedating property and cities: "here, where the pasture squelches underfoot / And England stirs, forever to hold my bones."

Sisson's lyricism, never self-indulgent, sometimes very pure, takes us into the heart of a rurally centered love of the displaced past, a love of things abandoned, renounced, all but forgotten. His tone, and even his thought, are not so different from, say, those of Frost's "Directive." And if I have suggested he is a kind of gnarled preacher, I regret it. Genuine poetry like his normalizes the subjective world, however initially alien to a reader, that it projects.

—M. L. Rosenthal

Selected Poems

On a Troopship

They are already made
Why should they go
Into boring society
Among the soldiery?
But I, whose imperfection
Is evident and admitted
Needing further assurance
Must year-long be pitted
Against fool and trooper
Practising my integrity
In awkward places,
Walking till I walk easily
Among uncomprehended faces
Extracting the root
Of the matter from the diverse engines
That in an oath, a gesture or a song
Inadequately approximate the human norm.

In Time of Famine: Bengal

I do not say this child
This child with grey mud
Plastering her rounded body
I do not say this child
For she walks poised and happy
But I say this
Who looks in at the carriage window
Her eyes are big
Too big
Her hair is touzled and her mouth is doubtful
And I say this
Who lies with open eyes upon the pavement
Can you hurt her?
Tread on those frightened eyes
Why should it frighten her to die?
This is a fault
This is a fault in which I have a part.

In a Dark Wood

Now I am forty I must lick my bruises
What has been suffered cannot be repaired
I have chosen what whoever grows up chooses
A sickening garbage that could not be shared.

My errors have been written in my senses
The body is a record of the mind
My touch is crusted with my past defences
Because my wit was dull my eye grows blind.

There is no credit in a long defection
And defect and defection are the same
I have no person fit for resurrection
Destroy then rather my half-eaten frame.

But that you will not do, for that were pardon
The bodies that you pardon you replace
And that you keep for those whom you will harden
To suffer in the hard rule of your Grace.

Christians on earth may have their bodies mended
By premonition of a heavenly state
But I, by grosser flesh from Grace defended,
Can never see, never communicate.

Sparrows Seen from an Office

You should not bicker while the sparrows fall
In chasing pairs from underneath the eaves
And yet you should not let this enraged fool
Win what he will because you fear his grief.

About your table three or four who beg
Bully or trade because those are the passions
Strong enough in them to hide all other lack
Sent to corrupt your heart or try your patience.

If you are gentle, it is because you are weak
If bold, it is the courage of a clown
And your smart enemies and you both seek
Ratiocination without love or reason.

O fell like lust, birds of morality
O sparrows, sparrows, sparrows whom none regards
Where men inhabit, look in here and see
The fury and cupidity of the heart.

A Duckling

I almost prayed for its departing
The tiny bird with sodden feathers
The Christian faith forbids such pity

The duckling weaker than her sisters
Crouching in straw within the hen-coop
Recedes from the immeasurable time.

So small a life with beady eye
Comfort cannot come at and none accompany
Entering among threshed ears the darkening shades.

Moriturus

The carcase that awaits the undertaker
But will not give up its small voice lies
Hollow and grim upon the bed.

What stirs in it is hardly life but a morosity
Which when this skipped as a child was already under
        the lids
Rebellious and parting from the flesh.

What drunken fury in adolescence pretended
Merely to possess the flesh and drove onwards
The blind soul to issue in the lap of Venus?

The hope of fatherhood, watching the babe sucking
(Ah, he will grow, hurled headlong into the tomb!)
Gives way to a tenderness spilt into amnesia.

The last chat of corruption reasonable as a syllogism
The image of God is clear, his love wordless
Untie my ligaments, let my bones disperse.

Family Fortunes

I

I was born in Bristol, and it is possible
To live harshly in that city

Quiet voices possess it, but the boy
Torn from the womb, cowers

Under a ceiling of cloud. Tramcars
Crash by or enter the mind

A barred room bore him, the backyard
Smooth as a snake-skin, yielded nothing

In the fringes of the town parsley and honeysuckle
Drenched the hedges.

II

My mother was born in West Kington
Where ford and bridge cross the river together

John Worlock farmed there, my grandfather
Within sight of the square church-tower

The rounded cart-horses shone like metal
My mother remembered their fine ribbons

She lies in the north now where the hills
Are pale green, and I

Whose hand never steadied a plough
Wish I had finished my long journey.

III

South of the march parts my father
Lies also, and the fell town

That cradles him now sheltered also
His first unconsciousness

He walked from farm to farm with a kit of tools
From clock to clock, and at the end

Only they spoke to him, he
Having tuned his youth to their hammers.

IV

I had two sisters, one I cannot speak of
For she died a child, and the sky was blue that day

The other lived to meet blindness
Groping upon the stairs, not admitting she could not see

Felled at last under a surgeon's hammer
Then left to rot, surgically

And I have a brother who, being alive
Does not need to be put in a poem.

In Honour of J.H. Fabre

My first trick was to clutch
At my mother and suck
Soon there was nothing to catch
But darkness and a lack.

My next trick was to know
Dividing the visible
Into shapes which now
Are no longer definable.

My third trick was to love
With the pretence of identity
Accepting without proof
The objects 'her' and 'me'.

My last trick was to believe
When I have the air
Of praying I at least
Join the mantis its prayers.

Cranmer

Cranmer was parson of this parish
And said Our Father beside barns
Where my grandfather worked without praying.

From the valley came the ring of metal
And the horses clopped down the track by the stream
As my mother saw them.

The Wiltshire voices floated up to him
How should they not overcome his proud Latin
With We depart answering his *Nunc Dimittis*?

One evening he came over the hillock
To the edge of the church-yard already filled with bones
And saw in the smithy his own fire burning.

Money

I was led into captivity by the bitch business
Not in love but in what seemed a physical necessity
And now I cannot even watch the spring
The itch for subsistence having become responsibility.

Money the she-devil comes to us under many veils
Tactful at first, calling herself beauty
Tear away this disguise, she proposes paternal solicitude
Assuming the dishonest face of duty.

Suddenly you are in bed with a screeching tear-sheet
This is money at last without her night-dress
Clutching you against her fallen udders and sharp bones
In an unscrupulous and deserved embrace.

Ellick Farm

The larks flew up like jack-in-the-boxes
From my moors, and the fields were edged with foxgloves.

The farm lay neatly within the hollow
The gables climbing, the barn beside the doorway.

If I had climbed into the loft I should have found a boy
Forty years back, among the bales of hay.

He would have known certainly all that I know
Seeing it in the muck-strewn cobbles below.

(Under the dark rim of the near wood
The tears gathered as under an eyelid.)

It would have surprised him to see a tall man
Who had travelled far, pretending to be him.

But that he should have been turning verses, half dumb
After half a lifetime, would least have surprised him.

The Un-Red Deer

The un-red deer
In the un-green forest

The antlers which do not appear
And are not like branches

The hounds which do not bay
With tails which do not swish

The heather beyond and the insignificant stumble
Of the horse not pulled up

By the rider who does not see all this
Nor hear nor smell it

Or does so but it does not matter
The horn sounds Gone away

Or, if it does not, is there hunter,
Hunted, or the broken tree

Swept by the wind from the channel?

Good-Day, Citizen

My life is given over to follies
More than I can exaggerate:
If I told you half you would imagine
That I am a very respectable person.

First, there is the folly of earning money
In order to have what is called independence:
You can admire that quality if you will,
I know what it is and do not admire it.

14

Secondly, there is the folly of spending it wisely,
So much for insurance, so much for the house,
Suitable provision for the children's education
Which for the most part they would rather not have.

Thirdly there would be, if that were not in fact all,
The supervening graces of domestic virtue
Everything paid up, honest as the day
But I am nearest to my own language in sleep.

The Nature of Man

It is the nature of man that puzzles me
As I walk from Saint James's Square to Charing Cross;
The polite mechanicals are going home,
I understand their condition and their loss.

Ape-like in that their box of wires
Is shut behind a face of human resemblance,
They favour a comic hat between their ears
And their monkey's tube is tucked inside their pants.

Language which is all our lies has us on a skewer,
Inept, weak, the grinning devil of comprehension; but sleep
Knows us for plants or undiscovered worlds;
If we have reasons, they lie deep.

A Letter to John Donne

On 27 July 1617, Donne preached at the parish church at Sevenoaks, of which he was rector, and was entertained at Knole, then the country residence of Richard Sackville, third Earl of Dorset.

I understand you well enough, John Donne
First, that you were a man of ability
Eaten by lust and by the love of God
Then, that you crossed the Sevenoaks High Street
As rector of Saint Nicholas:
I am of that parish.

To be a man of ability is not much
You may see them on the Sevenoaks platform any day
Eager men with despatch cases
Whom ambition drives as they drive the machine
Whom the certainty of meticulous operation
Pleasures as a morbid sex a heart of stone.

That you should have spent your time in the corruption of courts
As these in that of cities, gives you no place among us:
Ability is not even the game of a fool
But the click of a computer operating in a waste
Your cleverness is dismissed from the suit
Bring out your genitals and your theology.

What makes you familiar is this dual obsession;
Lust is not what the rutting stag knows
It is to take Eve's apple and to lose
The stag's paradisal look:
The love of God comes readily
To those who have most need.

You brought body and soul to this church
Walking there through the park alive with deer
But now what animal has climbed into your pulpit?
One whose pretension is that the fear
Of God has heated him into a spirit
An evaporated man no physical ill can hurt.

16

Well might you hesitate at the Latin gate
Seeing such apes denying the church of God:
I am grateful particularly that you were not a saint
But extravagant whether in bed or in your shroud.
You would understand that in the presence of folly
I am not sanctified but angry.

Come down and speak to the men of ability
On the Sevenoaks platform and tell them
That at your Saint Nicholas the faith
Is not exclusive in the fools it chooses
That the vain, the ambitious and the highly sexed
Are the natural prey of the incarnate Christ.

Easter

One good crucifixion and he rose from the dead
He knew better than to wait for age
To nibble his intellect
And depress his love.

Out in the desert the sun beats and the cactus
Prickles more fiercely than any in his wilderness
And his forty days
Were merely monastic.

What he did on the cross was no more
Than others have done for less reason
And the resurrection you could take for granted.

What is astonishing is that he came here at all
Where no one ever came voluntarily before.

Loquitur Senex

I return to the horror of truth
After a life of business:
I was happy to be employed
But now my hunger is extreme.

The swans drift by and the bridge
Is pendulous over the profound stream:
The water is habitable by the mind
And the stationary fish are swimming against it.

Where were the fish when I
Flurried by consultation,
Laboured to distinguish myself
In vanity and discursive reason?

Now, with the fish, nose pressed
Against reality,
I look through the watery glass
At weeds standing on stone.

The age is lost that had
Laughter hidden under the hand
But in the peace that remains
There is still what lives in the eye.

Gracious God, when the tension gives
And I am swept below the weir
Do as Berkeley says
Hold this world in your mind.

The Temple

Who are they talking to in the big temple?
If there were a reply it would be a conversation:
It is because there is none that they are fascinated.
What does not reply is the answer to prayer.

In Memoriam Cecil de Vall

late garrison chaplain, Barrackpore

You can count me as one who has hated
Out of spoiled love rather than malice.
Let me lie now between tufts of heather,
My head in the grass.

The sky is too high, I prefer to be far under it
The road is happily distant.
No angel shall catch me here, nor tourist
Abase me with his talk.

Out from this patch of dust the flat plain
Extends like Asia under a blue sky.
It is no misanthropy that binds me here
But recognition of my own failure.

I ask no better than that
The long convolvulus shall grow over me
And prickling gorse
Keep the children away.

Soon the fallen flesh will begin to crawl
Making off in the worm's belly
Into the undergrowth, and the polished flies
Will riddle me like hat-pins.

I bid their rising lives welcome because
It is better to be many than one;
The mirrors of blue-bottle and worm
May reflect to more purpose than I.

Curl my fin where the shark
Lurches in the blue Mediterranean;
Open my wizened eye
Like a lizard under a tropical leaf.

As I bite the dust of this flat land
For the last time, with dissolving chaps,
Keep me free from all such reflection
Lest the mind dazzle as it goes out.

I do not wish to recognise Christ
As I enter the shades.
What other company could I have
In darkness of my own choosing?

Perhaps it is no more than a recollection
– The banks of a river,
The heavy vegetation wet with the monsoon,
My friend on the verandah?

He brought out the long whiskies and proved
That God hated nothing that He had made:
At no time did I take at his hands
Any but his own hospitality.

Fill my mouth with sand, let the passer's boot
Unwittingly fold my skull.
I have resigned the pretensions
Of the individual will.

From the darkened shores of the river
The dogs howled;
I was alone with the famished and the dead.
Whatever stirred in those shadows was not God.

Christmas at the Greyhound

'All strangers now; there is nobody that I know.'
Draw near to the hearth; there is one nature of fire.

Virgini Senescens

I

Do you consider that I lied
Because I offered silent hands?

And are my lips no use at all
Unless they have a lie to tell?

Because my eyes look doubtfully
Must they not look on you at all?

And if my hands drop to my sides
Are they then empty of desire?

And are my legs unusable
Because the linked bones of my feet

Rest where they are upon the floor?
I could have used them otherwise

And brought my legs across the room,
Lifted my arms and caught you up

And housed my eyes under your brows
And fixed my lips upon your own.

Or would you then have said that I
Performed but did not speak the truth?

II

Although the body is your truth
The mind may have some part in it

As, mine that holds your body fast
And yours, said to keep house inside

Perhaps the yawning mind of God
Which folds us in his universe.

The mind that holds you is my eye
The quicksilver inside your own

Which, seeing me, collects and runs;
It is the mucous in my skull

And your intestines tight with fear
Our several secret, hirsute parts

Our finger-nails which dig the flesh;
It is our flushed or dented skin

The toes we clench inside our shoes.
Or do you think it less than that?

The spidery numbers you can read?
The tricks they play among themselves?

The art by which you hope to draw
A self from chaos, and be pleased?

A reputation? Who admires?
Oh, I am old and sly, I twist

A way through ribs and weeds and trees
And mark my body as I go:

While you are young, and hardly dare
Moisten your lips upon a stone,

Your fluttering look is hardly out
And does not reach your nearer parts.

Do not imagine I am bold.
It is this terror I admire:

It is the shaking universe
I too inhabit, but in me

Age has reformed the hope of love.
The *quia impossibile*

Drifts with me as, I make no doubt,
It travels with the astronaut.

III

I turn myself from you, to think
Upon the gravity of age

Which bears upon me now until
My weightless body floats in space.

I want it anchored where I live
Why should I bother with the mind?

It is an old excuse for death
Or else a young man's sleight-of-hand:

Attend to that and he will grow
And, silent as a savage, steal

Upon the world of sex and war.
He will grow up while I grow down

And hold you firmly in his arms
Still talking of the intellect

And, turning to me, will pretend
That we are equals in our minds

Although my body shrink until
He well could throw me out of doors

Or push my huddled frame against
The fender, while he pokes the fire.

It has not come to that, but I
Must plan now my civilities

While I can give him knock for knock.
I will accept his gambit and

Use all my thin and polished words
To make him feel my harmless ease

Whereas my burning heart prepares
To snatch you from him if I can.

It can do you no good, this war
In which you gain by my defeat.

Do not suppose I shall give up
Till I have hurt you if I can.

Iago was an honest man;
I have that reputation too.

In Allusion to Propertius, I, iii

When I opened the door she was asleep.
It is thus I imagine the scene, after Propertius.

The torches flickered all over the world
My legs staggered but I went to her bed

And let myself down gently beside her.
Her head was propped lightly upon her hands.

I passed one arm under her body
And with my free hand I arranged her hair

Not disturbing her sleep. She was Ariadne
Desolate upon the coast where Theseus had left her,

Andromeda, no longer chained to the rock,
In her first sleep. Or she was Io,

A milk-white heifer browsing upon her dreams,
I Argus, watching her with my hundred eyes.

I took kisses from her and drew my sword.
Then, through the open window the moon looked in:

It was the white rays opened her eyes.
I expected her to reproach me, and she did:

Why had I not come to her bed before?
I explained that I lived in the underworld

Among shadows. She had been in that forest.
Had we not met, she said, in that place?

Hand in hand we wandered among the tree-trunks
And came into the light at the edge of the forest.

Preface (Catullus)

Catullus walked in the Campus Martius.
He had seen all he needed to see,
Lain on his bed at noon, and got up to his whore.
His heart had been driven out of his side
By a young bitch – well, she was beautiful,
Even, while the illusion was with him, tender.
She had resolved herself into splayed legs
And lubricity in the most popular places.
He had seen Caesar who – had he not been, once,
The drunken pathic of the King of Bithynia? –
Returning in triumph from the western isles:
Nothing was too good for this unique emperor.
Against these fortunes he had nothing to offer
– Possibly the remains of his indignation,
A few verses that would outlive the century.
His mind was a clear lake in which he had swum:
There was nothing but to await a new cloud.
We have seen it. But Catullus did not;
He had already hovered his thirty years
On the edge of the Mediterranean basin.
The other, rising like a whirlwind in a remote province,

Was of a character he would have ignored.
And yet the body burnt out by lechery,
Turning to its tomb, was awaiting this,
Fore-running as surely as John the Baptist
An impossible love pincered from a human form.

Valediction (Catullus)

Catullus my friend across twenty centuries,
Anxious to complete your lechery before Christ came.

The Rope

Now money is the first of things
And after that the human heart
Which beats the time it can afford.
    What springs
  Of passion, what a smart
      Appearance, Lord!
And are these spiritual things?

They are. And we that are without
Have failed to use the currency
Correctly. For we have allowed
    A doubt
  About the things we see
    To sing aloud
And put our calculations out.

If the external is the hope
We have here, as I think it is,
We should respect it till we die.
    The slope
  Is steep, the precipice
    Is near. And I
Now know that money is the rope.

The Person

What is the person? Is it hope?
If so, there is no I in me.
    Is it a trope
Or paraphrase of deity?
    If so,
I may be what I do not know.

Do not be proud of consciousness
For happiness is in the skin.
    What you possess
Is what another travels in.
    Your light
Is phosphorus in another's night.

It does not matter what you say
For any what or who you are
    Is of a day
Which quite extinguishes your star –
    Not speech
But what your feelers cannot reach.

There is one God we do not know
Stretched on Orion for a cross
    And we below
In several sorts of lesser loss
    Are we
In number not identity.

The Regrets

I

Beware of age.
For I have learned
An old man should
Be kept in chains.
He is a gentle
Psychopath;
The passion that
He had is dead.
His youthful walk
And grey moustache
Conceal a heart
Which cannot feel.
The courtesy
Which he expends
Is poison to
His younger friends.
His virtues are
A kind of shell
To keep him cosy
In his skull.
I tell you mark
This leper well
And send him forward
With a bell.

II

Young men are fools
And now I am old
I am a fool.

III

Lust is the star
Which lit my way
And brought me close
To where you lay
– One wise man with

A pack of lies
Or not enough
To make him wise.
God's blood, they say,
Oozed from the tree.
The serpent sweated
Just like me
But in his more
Enlightened years
The devil was
A gentleman.

On my Fifty-First Birthday

I

Hare in the head-lights dance on your hind legs
Like a poor cat straggling at a rope's end.
Everything is cruelty for innocence.
If you could mark this escape from death
In your thin mind you would have eaten what I have
And, running from form to form, you would consider
The immeasurable benignity of the destructive God.

II

A great sunlit field full of lambs.
The distant perspectives are of the patched earth
With hedges creeping about. If I were to die now
No need of angels to carry me to paradise.
O Lord my God, simplify my existence.

III

The whole hill-side is roofed with lark-song.
What dangerous declivities may I not descend?
It is dark green where the horses feed.
Blackthorn and gorse open before my eyes.

The gulls come inland, alight on the brown land
And bring their sea-cries to this stillness.
It was waves and the surf running they heard before
And now the lark-song and the respiration of leaves.

Homo Sapiens is of No Importance

And it may be that we have no nature
That he could have taken upon him.
Plato of course discussed it.
Deborah sitting under a tree
In a time of matriarchy:
Blessed be thou among women,
Blessed be the hand, the hammer,
Blessed the tent-peg as it drove through Sisera,
Blessed the connection between two interiors,
Blessed the wire between the switch and the bulb.
Not for the mind of Jael but for her hand
Not for the hand but for the hammer
Not for the hammer but for the tent-peg
Not for the peg but for Sisera dead
Not for Sisera dead but for his army routed
Not for that but for the momentary ease under a tree
Not for that but for the tree itself
Not for the tree but for the sand blowing by it
If there was any nature it was in that.

Metamorphoses

I

Actaeon was a foolish hind
To run from what he had not seen.

He was a hunter, and had called
An end to slaughter for that day

And laid his weapons by a well.
Diana knew the man he was

But took her kirtle from her waist.
She gave her arrows to her maids

Then dropped her short and flimsy dress.
There was some muscle on the girl.

I think she knew the hunt was up
But set the hounds upon the man

To show her bitter virgin spite.
There was some blood but not her own.

Actaeon sped, his friends hallo'ed,
The forest rang but not with tears.

His favourite whippet bit his flank:
His friends hallo'ed him to the kill

Which they were sure he would enjoy.
Diana by the fountain still

Shuddered like the water on her flesh
And after that there came the night.

II

– Or else he was a rutting stag
Turned to a man because he saw

Diana bathing at the pool
– As you might turn a foreskin back.

III

Pygmalion was an artful man;
Sculpsit and pinxit were his trade.

He would not have a woman in
The confines of his silky bed;

The ones he knew were troublesome.
Still, he admired the female form

And cut another in that shape
But it was marble, rather hard.

He laid it down upon his bed
And drew a purple coverlet

Across its shapely breasts and legs.
However, it did not respond.

He got it up and gave it clothes
And brought it several sorts of toys.

It did not speak a single word
So in despair he said his prayers.

He did not even dare to say
'This marble' or 'this ivory';

He merely said he'd like a girl
Resembling one he'd made himself.

After his prayers the boy went home
And got back to his kissing game.

To his surprise the girl grew warm;
He slobbered and she slobbered back

– This is that famous mutual flame.
The worst of all was yet to come.

Although he often wished her back
In silent marble, good and cold

The bitch retained her human heat,
The conquest of a stone by art.

May Venus keep me from all hope
And let me turn my love to stone.

IV

O will you take a fluttering swan
Eurotas, on your plashy banks?

Where the dissimulating bird
Fled from a Venus he had coaxed

Into an eagle with a beak.
Eurotas showed beneath her waves

The rippling image of a girl.
She rose to take the frightened bird

And struggled with him to the bank.
It was the bird came out on top.

Its wings concealed the thing it did
But showed the fluttering legs and hands.

The bird became a stable thing:
There are such dangers for a girl.

Europa felt a sighing bull
Beside her, as she gathered flowers.

It was a gentle, milk-white beast
And tried to graze upon her hair.

She patted and embraced its neck;
Its breath grew deeper as she stroked.

At last she climbed upon his back,
One hand upon a stubby horn.

Over his broad and shaggy cloth
The creature felt the gentle limbs

And in a trice he was away.
Europa held the swimming beast;

She looked at the receding shore
And clutched her garments from the wind.

V

When Virgo crosses with the Ram
Expect a rain of falling stars,

A spilling cornucopia
Betokening plenty, but no peace,

A Danae in her open boat
The eleemosynary shower

That fell, can now get up again
And it is Easter in the world.

The first age was the age of gold;
The age of iron is our own.

VI

The day, the year, the century,
The glacial winter, and the spring

And then the naked summer brings
The rutting stag to the church door.

But first the Phaeton from the crown
Of heavens descends into the waves.

There was no reason in his course
And on his way he burnt the world

And when you visited the shades
Did you see my Eurydice,

Christ, on that terrifying day?
I sit beneath the pulpit for

The bitter, abnegated hour.
I have no notion what you did.

In manus tuas. Afterwards.
Except you walked three days in hell.

Was there dumb kindness in the shades?
Who is that nacreous figure there

The empty sunlight falls upon
Although there is no light to fall?

Will she resume the upper light?
And when you come to Thomas in

The confines of his doubting room
Was she left in an orange grove?

There was a garden. Calvary.
And Adam fell where you got up.

But was the resurrected flesh
Less tempted than the flesh of Eve?

The naked figure in the grove
Diana's or the risen Christ's?

Her altar or the flesh we eat?
The world is uncreated by

The death of him that made the world.
By the slain lamb there trots the fawn.

VII

Here are two stories of old men:
The virtuous Boaz is the first.

He lay upon the threshing floor
And dreamed of Ruth, who soon came in

And while in sleep he saw the fields
Where she had stooped to gather corn

She gently lifted, in the dark,
The rug that hid his bony toes.

It was a rather pleasant dream.
Benign and virtuous to himself

He wished he could be warm like Ruth.
And there she was. But he was scared.

He sent her home and merely bit
The aged spit upon his beard

And did it honestly next day.
As he was rich the world approved.

The second story is about
Two men whose desiccated years

Were sheltered in the splendid house
Of Joachim, a juicy lord.

They earned their keep by being just
But saw Susanna every day.

She was a soft and tender bit.
They noticed when she took her bath

And both devised a pleasant plan
To help her with the soap and rinse.

They waited in the garden where
She took it when the sun was hot.

Unhappily it warmed them too
And made them lie to get their way.

Then they were frightened and resumed
Their great pretence of being just.

Less fortunate than Boaz, they
Could only hope to have her killed

But even this did not come off
And Daniel had them cut in two.

VIII

Which otherwise might have been born.
They carried in a bloody tray

This unripe apple plucked within
The forest of the uterus.

This one at least will not arrive
At ages suitable for tears.

Within this forest everything
Begins. Although I may not say

Eurydice walks with her tears
It is the grove where they began.

It is the grove where I walked out,
Blind as upon my latest days.

I had a kind of folded life.
The butterfly with its wet wings

Has twice the power I had to fly.
And how then to the garden where

The loaded Tree of Knowledge stood?
Deceptively completed man

Beside a woman as complete?
No expectation in his eyes

His member like a falling leaf;
The fronded entrance to Eve's cave

Admitting no posterity.
The shining apples had no life.

Then how could Adam come to find
A tree more naked than himself,

Excoriate of leaves and fruit
And he himself nailed to the boughs?

Some serpent must have let him hope,
Which his glazed body could not do

Without hortation from a flesh
He had forgotten was his own.

Some spasm must have found its end
And broken his tumescent heart.

Eve must have let her children out
From her forced womb, to right and left.

But first, within, the spinning wave
Of sperm had sent its foam-flake out

To meet the southward-seeping egg
And this encounter did not hear

Either the paradisal speech
Exchanged when congress was agreed

Or the reared serpent's good advice
So soft that it became a hiss.

It needed Cain and Abel too,
The brothers Murder and Incite

And Noah with his upturned eyes,
Lifting his skirts out of the wet

And Abraham in fear of God,
Getting his holy cutlass out.

The sober, patriarchal life
In which the richest was the best

And now the surgeon with his smile
And sister's deferential cough.

IX

The metamorphosis of all.
Or he was nothing but a child

Magi attended for the star
And shepherds for their singing ears.

Funny how he became a Mass,
To eat his body, when he died,

The first essay of carpentry
Building an ark for the whole world

As you might nail a coffin up.
The golden age began anew;

What had been first became the last.
Declension to the age of iron

Was unimportant after all.
And yet there must remain a doubt.

The giants piling up the sky,
Pelion on Ossa, also rose

And what will rise must also fall.
We know it by experience.

It is the waning of the year.
A death in spring-time is the best.

The Consequence

I

There is no more to say than No
And Nothing is my farthest end.
A man has pity for his friend
But I am only glad to go.
Now therefore let the handsome crow
Pick out the eyes I would not lend.

II

We feed on death for half our lives
But vomit when we let it in.
The final pallor of the skin
Betokens that the patient thrives.
How earnestly the swimmer dives!
How eager his returning fin!

III

Old age protects itself with hope
And leans to suck the kiss of youth.
How kindly Boaz took to Ruth!
The lion with the antelope.
And what delighted fingers grope
In cradles to forget the truth!

IV

But there is twilight and the rose
And other such ephemera.
The crocus and Proserpina
Distract us to a brief repose.
And I, who have a polished heart,
Harder than any sympathy
But excellent for lechery
Or any sanctimonious part
For ever leave the truth alone;
It crunches time up like a stone
While love, the centre of the mind
Nibbles the flesh from head to feet.
The dusty streets of Sodom find
Two constables upon the beat.

V

Plato, whom reason ate like sex,
Preferred the form before the thing.
But what contentment did that bring?
Whom did that ever unperplex?
Meanwhile incessant number pecks
At form, until the scaffolding
Of all our thoughts is down, to fling
The gates of chaos on our necks.
Judas went out and hanged himself
And so should I, for I am he.
There is no Adam to set free.

VI

The forest of a long intent
Has tracks where I may lose my way
Nor was the place I am today
Intended by the way I went.
The night has only disarray;
It does not see what day mistook.
What was it that the nightmare shook?
Although I heard the drum today
The same occasions day by day

Provide me with identity.
I do what the occasions say
For nothing never is without
The thing it wants, and for its play
A futile gesture is the best.

Evening

Sleep has my muscles and a cord my throat.
Faint heart! The rooks at evening repair,
Climbing upon so many steps on air,
To the elm tops; caw, on the balustrade,
Caw from the church-tower, where the dead are laid
Under a passing shadow. I to tea,
Beside the fire in the old house, quietly.

Aller Church

The art, the artifex, and I.
        Let the wind blow softly.
Currents of air over the plain.
        When shall I see England again?
The mouse creeps in the sedge. The fire runs
        Over the stubble against the sun.
This world is not yours. Walk here
        Under the half edge of Sedgemoor.

The Usk

Christ is the language which we speak to God
And also God, so that we speak in truth;
He in us, we in him, speaking
To one another, to him, the City of God.

I

Such a fool as I am you had better ignore
Tongue twist, malevolent, fat mouthed
I have no language but that other one
His the Devil's, no mouse I, creeping out of the cheese
With a peaked cap scanning the distance
Looking for truth.
Words when I have them, come out, the Devil
Encouraging, grinning from the other side of the street
And my tears
Streaming, a blubbered face, when I am not laughing
Where in all this
Is calm, measure,
Exactness
The Lord's peace?

II

Nothing is in my own voice because I have not
Any. Nothing in my own name
Here inscribed on water, nothing but flow
A ripple, outwards. Standing beside the Usk
You flow like truth, river, I will get in
Over me, through me perhaps, river let me by crystalline
As I shall not be, shivering upon the bank.
A swan passed. So is it, the surface, sometimes
Benign like a mirror, but not I passing, the bird.

III

Under the bridge, meet reward, the water
Falling in cascades or worse, you devil, for truthfulness
Is no part of the illusion, the clear sky
Is not yours, the water
Falling not yours
Only the sheep
Munching at the river brim
Perhaps

IV

What I had hoped for, the clear line
Tremulous like water but
Clear also to the stones underneath
Has not come that way, for my truth
Was not public enough, nor perhaps true.
Holy Father, Almighty God
Stop me before I speak

                    – *per Christum.*

V

Lies on my tongue. Get up and bolt the door
For I am coming not to be believed
The messenger of anything I say.
So I am come, stand in the cold tonight
The servant of the grain upon my tongue,
Beware, I am the man, and let me in.

VI

So speech is treasured, for the things it gives
Which I can not have, for I speak too plain
Yet not so plain as to be understood
It is confusion and a madman's tongue.
Where drops the reason, there is no one by.
Torture my mind: and so swim through the night
As envy cannot touch you, or myself

Sleep comes, and let her, warm at my side, like death.
The Holy Spirit and the Holy One
Of Israel be my guide. So among tombs
Truth may be sought, and found, if we rejoice
With Ham and Shem and Japhet in the dark
The ark rolls onward over a wide sea.
Come sleep, come lightning, comes the dove at last.

In Spring-Time

Another time, this way the primrose,
I lost my way before my age was full
In a deep valley. And the cleft said nothing
But perhaps, I am limestone, grey
Lichen upon me, grey.

No voice. Came summer yet no voice. Came once
The lark, the plover and the hare in March.
Almost the wind is speech.

What turns I took and then the cock-crow came
Not once but many times.

Sumptuary Laws

Still with the hope of being understood,
Of understanding myself
Or understanding someone else,
I engaged in restless action.
It was no good.
First because
It had no issue, secondly because
If it could have had, I would no longer care.
The problems of age are semblant, one thing
Like another, no thing identical,
The things having been seen, the passions

Expended in better times by a better man.
So outwardly and above
We turn, gracious and empty
The old hypocrites, counting the stars,
Loving the children, counting them like money.
Thanking what stars we have that the wrong turnings
Have all been taken, a life of comfort
Assured, as it may be, to the last deception
I could call this life respectable but
I must call it mine, which is worse.

Somerton Moor

I

You are unusual, but the touch
Of innocence may sear a mind.
I know who say so, for I am
The prisoner of a loving ghost

O death, come quickly, for the fiend
Crosses the marshes with my tears.

II

Under the peat, dark mystery of earth,
Fire of the hearth, enchanter of my heart
The smoke that rises is a sacrifice
The peat moves over in its sodden sleep

And I, who should have touched her with my wand
Let her evade beneath the burning turf
And now through smoke and bitterness I speak
Words she would recognise and no one else
And she can no more hear than oyster-ears.

III

Last speech. Accustomed as I am to speech
And she to silence, excellence is hard
For nothing that is facile can be heard
And nothing hard can be endured for long.
So sleep. Pass out between the willow-boughs
Out of my dream into the cool of death.
There, where the resurrection that you hope,
Though tardy, comes at last
The instrument I carry is untuned.

In Insula Avalonia

I

Huge bodies driven on the shore by sleep
The mountain-woman rocks might fall upon
And in the cavity the heaped-up man.

Sleep on the island like a witty zone
Seas break about it, frolicking like youth
But in the mists are eyes, not dancers, found.

Hurt is the shepherd on the inland hill
He has a cot, a staff and certain sheep
Stones are his bed, his tables and his bread.

This is not where the sirens were, I think
But somewhere, over there, the next approach
Behind that other island in the mist.

That was the song, beyond the linnet-call
At the cliff's edge, below the plunging gull
The fish it found, the enemy or Christ.

II

Counting up all the ways I have been a fool,
In the long night, although the convent clock
Winds several hours around Medusa's locks,

Geryon and Chrysaor are with me now
– Sure there was bad blood in that family –
And yet the worst of all was done by love.

The fool: but not the bow and naked babe
But top-coat murderers with sullen looks
And yet Medusa was a temple harlot.

Under the river-bank a seeping wind
Ripples the bubbles from a passing fish
No colder memory than gloomy Dis.

Look, for you must, upon the fine appearance,
The creature had it and is formless dead.
Now come no nearer than to straws in glass.

III

Dark wind, dark wind that makes the river black
– Two swans upon it are the serpent's eyes –
Wind through the meadows as you twist your heart.

Twisted are trees, especially this oak
Which stands with all its leaves throughout the year;
There is no Autumn for its golden boughs

But Winter always and the lowering sky
That hangs its blanket lower than the earth
Which we are under in this Advent-tide.

Not even ghosts. The banks are desolate
With shallow snow between the matted grass
Home of the dead but there is no one here.

What is a church-bell in this empty time?
The geese come honking in a careless skein
Sliding between the mort plain and the sky.

What augury? Or is there any such?
They pass over the oak and leave me there
Not even choosing, by the serpent's head.

IV

O there are summer riders
On the plain
                    in file or two by two

It is a dream

For Winter, one by one, is wringing us
The withers, one, and scrotum-tight the other

Yet I am here
Looking down on the plain, my elbow on
The sill

From which I night by night and day by day
Watch
                for the moon pours swimmingly

Upon this field, this stream
That feeds my sleep.

Be night
Be young
The morning half begun
Palls on the waiting mind and makes it scream

O Minnich, Minnich

Who is the lady there by Arthur's lake?
None is. A willow and a tuft of grass
But over bones it broods, as over mine
Somewhere
Except
            nowhere

Bind up your temples and begone from here
No need to answer. What is there to fear?

Only the wind that soughs, and soughs, and soughs.
Some say it does, and others contradict
Some say sleep strengthens, others that it kills
This music comes
                    from Wendover I think
Where meaning is at least, there, sure, am I.

V

Out in the sunlight there I am afraid
For dark depends upon the nascent mind
The light, the envy and the world at large

A field for flood, and fish and such-like deer
The willows standing in between the pools
Great siege this morning, in the morning-time

The water rustles like a turning page
Write then who will, but write upon the stream
Which passes nonchalantly through the hedge

No word of mine will ever reach the sea
For mine and words are clean contrary things
Stop here for envy, go there for your love

For love of persons are the passing geese
Swans on the flood, the dopping water-fowl
The cloud that cumbers while the sky is blue.

Awful at nights, the mind is blue today
Enlarged without a purpose like a lake
For purpose pricks the bubble of our thoughts.

Climb back to sleep, the savage in that mine
Picks with his teeth and leaves his skull to dry
O skull and cross-bones on the earthen floor

My earth, my water, my redundant trees
Breaking the surface like a stitch in skin.
No word but weather, let me be like that.

VI

A ruminant in darkness. So am I
Between the skin and half a hope of hell
Tell me till morning where the savage stops.

His eyes beside the fire. The burning peat
Is quiet, quiet, quiet till it shrieks
Not what the hammer was but what it says

The eyes on Thursday and the mind that waits
For sabbaths of intent but does no thing
Not seeking, waiting for a peaceful end

What wind is in the trees? What water laps
Extravagantly round the seeping hedge?
A house on sticks, where several yearned before

The skin, the furze, the movement into sleep
The watery lids beside the river bank
Mirrors of emptiness, O what way in?

VII

A mine of mind, descend who can that way
As down a staircase of the inner ring
Where figures are at liberty, and play

A plain of ghosts, among the rest a girl
(And none had touched her, though the serpent's teeth
Met in her heel below the flying skirt)

She gathered flowers, exacting from their grace
An outward parallel for grace of skin,
Petals for fingers, petals for arms and legs.

This transient surface is the thing I seek
No more, perhaps, than scale upon the eyes
Do not walk with her, winds are blown that way

A storm of leaves and all may disappear
And yet below the circle of my mind
Playing in spring-time there is Proserpine.

But I am rather Cerberus than Dis
Neither receive nor yet pursue this child
Nor am I Orpheus who could bring her back.

I stand and roar and only shake my chain
The river passes and gives others sleep
I am the jaws nothing will pass between.

VIII

The mind beyond the reach of human time
Mine or another's, let me now perceive
Time has turned sour upon the earth for me

A little earth, walking upon the earth
A molehill, Mother, on your credent slopes
But moving, time against me, everywhere

This is the lump out of which I was made
The hands, the feet, the brain no less is mud
What does not crumble must remain in shape

The shape of man, but moles are better off
Boring the hill-side like a nit in cheese
They asked for blindness, that is what they have

But I for light, for sleep, for anything
Moving my hands across the surfaced world
Exacerbate in darkness, though alive

I never came from any natural thing
To take this shape which is not mine at all
Yet I am I am I and nothing more

If any took this shape I took this shape
Yet taking what I did not ask to have
And being nothing till I took this shape

The shape of shafts of light and falling suns
Meteors incarcerate in balls of mud
A cracked example of a better kind

Admit you came because you could not know
Walk in the garden as you did one day
And if you cannot flatter, answer back.

IX

Some seek examples in the world of sense
They slide across the retina like dreams
Yet are objective in the world of deeps

Which swimmers may attempt, that move all ways
Across the current, from the pebbly floor
Up to the surface where the morning breaks

If any capture what the water-weed
Holds brightly like a bubble on its stem
Or what may disappear in lengthening dark

Volumes of sleep will turn the swimmer's arm
His leg will gently bump the feathered rock
Gulls cry above, sleep has no place for them

A call, a cry, a murder in the street
Is sign of others lonely as yourself
The Lord have mercy, others may as well.

X

I do not know and cannot know indeed
And do not want a word to tell me so
A sentence is construction more than I.

I feel, I vomit. I am left to earth
To trample and be trampled, in my turn
But always rotting from the day I came

Thy kingdom come. And could I pray indeed
I would be höhnisch and destroy the world
This is not what is meant and nor am I.

So let my silence fasten on a rock
Be lichen, that is plenty, for my mind
And not be where I was. Where is he? Gone

The empty space is better than himself
But best of all when, certain winters past,
No one says: There he was, I knew him well.

Martigues

I

Myrtle, roses and thyme
And the rose laurel:
I too have something that I wish to forget
There, where the woodland path
Passes into the concrete
And my tears are for a master.
At the gate I picked a leaf of laurel and said:
Dante
Wore these pointed leaves.
Here, in the bitter south,
A madman, between gaolers.
Whisper it to the myrtles we may, crushing the past
In our tingling fingers,
Or picking the thyme.
But the rose laurel

It is all I have, the bitten past,
Not all I came to.
Speeches were made and names taken, the heart
Burst out of his side.
No love like the unspoken
Ferocity, the bitter tears, a battle

Standing instead with brimming eyes
Looking out over the *étang*
The poverty of a few fish
And a garden of roses.

I too have something that I wish to forget.
Myrtle and roses, the same.
Controversy among apes is no custom
And my limbs fell hard
Against the rail of the scuttled ship. You may cup your eye-balls
For ordinary uses now.
My faith
Sprang into the air with indignation.

II

At the corner of the streets
The fishermen stand in groups
With brown faces: they have them from the Moors
And the wind blowing across the *étang*.

In the garden
Pierre, or perhaps Adam.
I shake him by the hand, brown also,
A fisherman's face, gardener's rather.
Help us with the language of saints.
Adam spoke
Softly, and in the old *patois*,
Knowing no other.
Myrtle, roses and thyme
And the rose laurel
Never to be let go.
I took him by the hand
Old friend
Whom I have never seen
Your ghost is my beginning, I have tears
For what is here forgotten
And in the winter of my age my hand
Cut the air with scimitars.

III

Roses and thyme
But leave the myrtle, leave the myrtle here
Roses and thyme
Fed on a garden where I made my home
And southward facing over the *étang*.
In Somerset I crumble up the soil
And linger on a terrace looking south
So minds have ears no voices
They have eyes
Which look upon the land and do no harm
But avarice is cupid in this game.
Yet love came after all, olive and rush,
The tart wine held under the cupping hand.
One taste of death. Good-night to all this lake.
The olives in the garden after all
Eat up the man and put him under ground
How should he turn his hand?

IV

Pallas Athene, wisdom in all this,
Mistress of olives and the curling prow
Let not your lids drop on this falling earth.
Set enmities at rest or let there be
Sufficient enmity to stir up love
And bring the sword before you bring smooth tongues,
Harsh enmities are best
And Judas put his silver in the ground.

V

Night falls, perhaps, upon my wide *étang*,
Joseph of Arimethea riding home.
The Saintes Maries
Await another pilgrim at this time
But now must sleep. And did he sleep or wake
Who walked upon this terrace in his dream?
The Saintes Maries put out their lights at last
And Joseph's ship touches a barren stone.

VI

He took a flower
And gave it in a morning without hope.
Hand down the rose
Hand down the myrtle, stuff the air with thyme.
There in a garden where it all began
Seek nothing for yourself. Seek nothing more
Than time will offer to dishonesty
And patience and the like. Silence at last
And Abraham's voice seeps through the air.
David is King. And then the dragons come
The thud of horses over the Camargue,
But silence first. The rose,
Myrtle crushed in the hand
And the rose laurel.

Marcus Aurelius

I do not want to pour out my heart any more
Like a nightingale bursting or a tap dripping:
Father no more verses on me, Marcus Aurelius
I will be an emperor and think like you.

Quiet, dignified, stretched out under a clothes line
The garden of my soul is open for inspection
As the gardener left it, chaque cheveu à sa place
And if you do not believe me you can comb through my papers
    yourself.

Of course you may not agree with: No hurt because the lips are
    tight.
The psychologists have been too much for you, but that rascal
    Freud
Did nothing but devise his own superficial entanglements
For his readers to trip over, while he smiled.

Old devil of Vienna, moving among the porcelain,
You were the beetle under the ruins of an empire
And where the Habsburgs had protruded their lips
You pinched your nostrils.

If I were a plain man I would do the same,
Dexterous, money-making, conforming to another pattern
Than the one I seek which will cover me entirely:
I hope to be an emperor under my own mausoleum.

Gardening

What night, corrupt, as this must be, with dreams
Gathers around this age and finds me now
Here in this garden, not in Eden, no
Another garden and another time

But there is neither slope nor sun can make
Amends for what I missed under your hands.
Old fool. Reproaches I could buy for nothing
In any market-place. How can I turn
This ageing sorrow to a biting wind
To catch me like the tangles of your hair

Gone and imagined? How can I turn
This burrow in the crumbling earth to peace?
Like a worm under stone. Or like a beetle
Making away and does not understand
Its movements, passions, parts.

Eastville Park

I sat on a bench in Eastville Park
It was Monday the 28th of October
I am your old intentions she said
And all your old intentions are over.

She stood beside me, I did not see her
Her shadow fell on Eastville Park
Not precise or shapely but spreading outwards
On the tatty grass of Eastville Park.

A swan might buckle its yellow beak
With the black of its eye and the black of its mouth
In a shepherd's crook, or the elms impend
Nothing of this could be said aloud.

I did not then sit on a bench
I was a shadow under a tree
I was a leaf the wind carried
Around the edge of the football game.

No need for any return for I find
Myself where I left myself – in the lurch
There are no trams but I remember them
Wherever I went I came here first.

Over the Wall
Berlin, May 1975

I

He will go over and tell the king
Or whoever is top dog in that country
How there is feasting here, the wastes are empty
The nine governors sleeping

Not a prophetic sleep, with the lids opening
Upon passion, dreaming of conflict

But the eyes turned inwards so that the whites
Gaze upon the world, and the heart ticks steadily
To the combustion of a strange engine
Not in the heart, more like a bee
Buzzing in the neighbourhood. Lost heart, lost head
There is no reflection under the cool brain
Which thinks only of last night's dominoes,
Glibly at least. Over the wall,
Knives drawn, teeth drawn back,
Swallowing the rattle they make in case the night
Should interpret their wishes.
Here in the west, far west, slumber
While death collects his paces.

I am not warlike but, once the frontiers are falling
Each man must put on his belt, it has been done before
And the whimpering must stop, Death being the kingdom
Of this world.

II

I have seen the doomed city, it was not my own
Love has no city like this, with barred hatreds
All bitterness, all shames. I do not think there is any
Feast to be eaten or long shawls
Trailed in the dust before the fanatic mob
Only quiet people live here, eating their sandwiches
Under the lilac while the boats go by,
Interminable imitation of reality
Which is not to be had, and should the frost fall
Should the eagle turn its head
The city of too many desperate adventures
I have seen them all, or so it seems, the Uhlans...
And now from the steppes
It is as if the Sarmatian horsemen came back,
Yet they do not stir, or make themselves visible...
One street I remember
There is no majesty in its lost endeavours
Speak to me no more, I have heard only
The marching men.
Sleep comes to those who deserve
Funerals under the chipped archways.

III

I do not think this is the end of the story
There are battalions enough behind the wall.
The tall policeman bent over me like the priest
Of an evil religion, as if I were the elements
And he the emissary who was empowered to transform me.
That was not the same
Dream-ridden solitude I had known before
Where a flame climbed the walls there was no one by.

IV

I know only aspen, beech, oak
But here on these wastes the turtle
Sang among the sands, sitting upon a pine-tree
No man has meditated this regress
Yet the afternoon sun falls upon faces
Less tame than tigers.

Est in Conspectu Tenedos

I

The day goes slowly, it is the first day
After the fall of Troy. I walk upon the beaches,
A ghost among ghosts, but the most shadowy I
O Tenedos O the thin island
Hiding the ships. They need not hide from me
I am the least figure upon the shore,
Which the wind does not notice, the water refract, or the
       sands count
As one of their number. I was a warrior,
Yes, in Troy
Before all reason was lost.
Where did Helen come from? Where is she now?
All reason is lost and so is she.
I was only a parcel of her reason

Now of her loss
Ghosts
Cannot be companionable; parts, shreds,
All that I am, ghost of a part of a part

II

Desolate shore, dark night
I have lost so much that I am not now myself
That lost it, I am the broken wind
The lost eagle flying, the dawn
Rising over Tenedos

III

Not any more I, that is the last thing
Rise or fall, sunrise or sunset
It is all one. The moon is not friendly
No, nor the sun
Nor darkness, nor
Even the bands of maidens bringing offerings
Pouring libations, buried
Among the ineluctable dead.

IV

Dead, ineluctable, certain
The fate of all men.

Reason

Reason had a pair of shoes
But quickly wore them out;
The uppers still looked very well
But, underneath, was doubt.

Of course, that let the water in,
And then it let in stones:
They skinned her feet; the flesh was thin,
And soon, she walked on bones.

Why not? But now, the trouble is
The joints are working loose.
At what point will the girl admit
You can be too abstruse?

Moon-Rise

It is the evening brought me here,
Or I the evening.
So I, which is the writing finger,
The hand placed on the sill, the night
Coming up from beyond Kingsbury:

Another foot, or hand, perhaps,
Perhaps a train, passing along
Down the line by the signal-box;
Or that rising star which may be
The next to come out of the west.
Which way? has no meaning because
Here and there relate to what:
The moon rises, as we say.

Nightingale, you sing no more;
The tree you sat on is not there;
The night you sang has also gone:
And I alone remember you,
Or am the nightingale tonight.

Night of the day, because succeeding;
Or of the night, because pleading;
Or of the Lamb of God because
Bleeding.
Useless to ask any question of
This night or any:
Answer as lightly as you ask.

The Herb-Garden

When a stream ran across my path
I stopped, dazzled, though the sparkle was at my feet;
The blind head moving forward, Gulliver
Walking toweringly over the little people.

Not that smaller in size meant, in any way, lesser;
It was merely that I could not see them, my eyes
Crunched on them as if they had been pebbles,
And I blundering without understanding.

Large is inept: how my loping arms fall,
The hands not prehensile, perpendicular
Before an inclined trunk. The legs do the damage,
Like the will of God without rhyme or reason.

Epithalamia are dreamed in this atmosphere
Which towers like a blue fastness over my head.
My head is full of rumours, but the perceptions
Dry like lavender within my skull.

Herb-garden, dream, scent of rosemary,
Scent of thyme, the deep error of sage,
Fennel that falls like a fountain, rue that says nothing,
Blue leaves, in a garden of green.

The Red Admiral

The wings tremble, it is the red admiral
Ecstatically against the garden wall;
September is his enjoyment, but he does not know it,
Name it, or refer to it at all.

The old light fades upon the old stones;
The day is old: how is there such light
From grey clouds? It is the autumnal equinox,
And we shall all have shrunk before daylight.

A woman, a horse and a walnut-tree: old voices
Out of recessed time, in the cracks,
It may be, where the plaster has crumbled:
But the butterfly hugs the blue lias.

The mystery is only the close of day,
Remembered love, which is also present:
Layer upon layer, old times, the fish turning
Once more in the pond, and the absent.

All could not be at once without memory
Crowding out what cannot be remembered;
Better to have none, best of all when
The evening sunlight has ended.

Its finger lighter than spiders, the red admiral
Considers, as I do, with little movement;
With little of anything that is meant:
But let the meaning go, movement is all.

Narcissus

corpus putat esse, quod umbra est

If I could only find a little stream
Which leapt out of the ground over black pebbles
And wore a hat of light on every ripple,
I should not care for the imaginary
Problems if I and Me, or Who or Why.
This corner of the world would be my mind;
What it saw I would say, if it were cloud,
Blue sky or even wind told by an eddy:
But what I would not see is this body,
Aged, severe, and, written on it, REFUSE.
If that came back into my little stream
It might be I should wake shrieking from my dream.
To what? Ah, what is there for us to wake to?
When pain is past, that is our hope or pleasure.
But nail that nothing now, keep me in vain
Beside the water, not seeing any shadow,
Only translucence, only the pebbles and earth,
A weed swaying, a fish, but nothing human
Or bearing any resemblance to man or woman,
Nothing compels our nature to this shape
For a stone will resemble the friends we make.
The mind is not peculiarly under skin
But might lie loose upon a high mountain.
A corner of a cloud would do for mind,
The bright border perhaps, with the moon behind,
The wind, recognized by its wandering billow
Scattering to surf as the moon comes and goes.
I thought I was a man because I was taught so.

Autumn Poems

En rond, nous sommes en rond
Ainsi, nous danserons.

I

The plunging year, the bright year. Through the clouds
Comes sunlight, sunlight, making iron-grey
The under-belly of the cloud it comes from.
Golden the dull leaves September wants to turn,
But dust is everywhere, not free, but plastered
Thinly over road, pavements, even bark
Branches and leaves, and the old iron buildings,
Ochre walls, fall. Not so, and yet it seems so.
Dust is the country way and dust the rhyme
Which equals everything in this sad time.

II

Broken-backed willow, elder and the sharp tree
Which is loaded with berries presently,
Heap upon heap, hawthorn, while the rose-hip
Beside her offers me her paler lip.

III

The world which was not mine, should I have wanted it?
By eating deceived, as Adam was,
I tell myself, but I do not believe it:
Belief is difficult after sixty years.

IV

Once there was bitterness which had regret in it
Or even hope, now there is none of these;
The bitterness itself is muted,
Not by satisfaction, which is not
But by etiolation, defoliation, the leaves
Growing whiter and thinner, and no wind through them.

Once I found sleep, it was
In the hollow of anybody else's hand
As the world sleeps in God's; now there is waking:
Not to receive the world, as some do,
But to watch, as the old, suspiciously.

I am looking for contentment out of nothing
For new things are made out of what is new
And I have none except this: the birds' song,
The rain, the evening sky, the grass on the lawn.

V

I am a tree: mark how the leaves grow
Sparsely now; here a bunch, there,
At the end of this thin twig, another
And the bark hardening, thickening. I am allowed
No respite from the wind, the long
Thorn trunk and branches stretching like a swan's neck
In torment. And the hiss
My own malice makes of this wind
Gentle enough, in itself: I can imagine myself
As this tree but what consciousness
Should go with it – that,
Screeching neck, I am blind to.

In Flood

A word for everybody, myself nobody,
Hardly a ripple over the wide mere:
There is the winter sunshine over the water,
The spirits everywhere, myself here.

Do you know it? It is Arthur's territory
– Agravaine, Mordred, Guinevere and Igraine –
Do you hear them? Or see them in the distant sparkle?
Likely not, but they are there all the same.

And I who am here, actually and statistically,
Have a wide absence as I look at the sea,
– Waters which 'wap and wan', Malory said –
And the battle-pile of those he accounted dead.

Yet his word breathes still upon the ripple
Which is innumerable but, more like a leaf
Curled in autumn and blown through the winter,
I on this hillside take my last of life:

Only glad that when I go to join them
I shall be speechless, no one will ask my name,
Yet among the named dead I shall be gathered,
Speaking to no man, not spoken to, but in place.

Waking

May has her beauties like another month,
Even June has her pleasures. I lie here,
The insistent thrust does not trouble me
Nor the slight breeze: a tree stump looks like a cat.
Yet all is not altogether well
Because of memory; crowd round me here
Rather, you ghosts who are to drink of Lethe.
Who else would go back to the upper world
Or take again the nerve-strings of the body
Or will to suffer grief and fear again?
Once I did: and the echo still comes back,
Not from the past only – which I could bear –
But from the young who set out hopefully
To find a bitter end where they began
And evil with the face of charity.
I have seen some such and do not want
Ever to pass along that road again
Where blind beggars hold out their hands for coin
And saints spit in their palms. This I have seen
And shall see if I wake from sleeping now.

The Absence

How can it be that you are gone from me,
Everyone in the world? Yet it is so,
The distance grows and yet I do not move.
Is it I streaming away and, if so, where?
And how do I travel from all equally
Yet not recede from where I stand pat
In the daily house or in the daily garden
Or where I travel on the motor-way?
Good-bye, good-bye all, I call out.
The answer that comes back is always fainter;
In the end those to whom one cannot speak
Cannot be heard, and that is my condition.
Soon there will be only wind and waves,
Trees talking among themselves, a chuchotement,
I there as dust, and if I do not reach
The outer shell of the world, still I may
Enter into the substance of a leaf.

The Hare

I saw a hare jump across a ditch:
It came to the edge, thought, and then went over
Five feet at least over the new-cut rhine
And then away, sideways, as if thrown
– Across the field where Gordon and I walked
Talking of apples, prices and bog-oak,
Denizens of the country, were it not
That denizens do not belong, as they do
And the hare tossing herself here and there.
And I? If I could, I would go back
To where Combe Farm stood, as Gordon's stands
Trenched in antiquity and looking out
Over immense acres not its own
And none the worse for that. You may say
It is the sick dream of an ageing man
Looking out over a past not his own.
But I say this: it is there I belong,

Or here, where the pasture squelches underfoot
And England stirs, forever to hold my bones.
You may boast of the city, I do not say
That it is not all you say it is
But at the Last Judgment it will stand
Abject before the power of this land.

Things

It is unbuilding now,
All I have to do
– Down, down and down.
It did not matter, no.

A man should have a thought
Or so I thought
But why did I think that?
I suppose, caught

By time and place
By a name or by a face.
Why not? For then and there
That was my case.

Things rule, O.K.? The mind
Is left behind:
Dazed and amazed, numb
Not, alas, blind.

Conscience

For any man whose words are sold
Will sell his conscience with his words:
The more he sells, so we are told,
The more the rascal should be heard.

It may be so, for humankind
Loves a cheat at a market-stall
Rattling his wares, although it finds
The goods are worth nothing at all.

Sisson's Good-Night

Goodnight, and hang me on a tree
Or lead me to the firing squad:
Say, he pretended once to be
The patriot and the friend of God.
It is not quite so bad as that,
But once I dabbled in the Creed
And England always has my love
– Two eccentricities indeed
But hardly capital offences
One would have thought, though there are those,
Certainly, whom they do not please
And the displeasure rather grows
Than lessens, in this world in which
I find myself septuagenarian:
Politics side with poor or rich
And all the Christians are Arian.
What did I say in all that ink
I spilt in poems, in novels or
The prose in which men say they think?
What was all that effusion for?
Hard to say: if it has a meaning
The words are there, you can find out
And you will find the author leaning
To too much hope or too much doubt

– Sometimes, they say, to plain despair;
More often, I would say, observing,
Quite simply, certain things are there
And that is more or less deserving
As others think they are there too
– And that includes the dead, as well
As critics A and B, or you,
And how right you are, time will tell.

Taxila

There is a rail-head at Havelian
– Or was, for I was there long ago –
Around it a sweet plain circled by hills:
This was my Greece, the only one I know.

It was a ghost of olives that I saw:
I had not seen the Mediterranean light
Where it falls, but I had dreamed of it.
I who had not been born woke to the sight.

Rus in urbe, urbs in the dazzling grey
– Or was it green? – green, but so grey and brown,
A spot of light in the surrounding darkness:
Taxila was the name of the town,

The heart of all I loved and could not have;
And in that limy track, as I approached,
A child with bright eyes offered a coin.
It was a bargain that was proposed.

Would I, the soldier of an alien army,
Neither the first nor the last to come that way,
Purchase for rupees certain disused drachmas
Left by the army of an earlier day?

Alexander himself came down from those hills,
Over the mountains beyond them to the north
– Far lands, the boy said, but mine was farther
And longer ago still my setting forth

For my exile burned me like the sun.
I should have bought that coin, I often thought of it
After that time, and in far different places:
It would have carried me over the Styx.

I would have returned, but there is no returning.
Yet you may rise, ghosts, or I sink to you.
The world is in my hand, breathing at last
For now I know, only the past is true.

The Christmas Rose

A spray of myrtle and the Christmas roses
Come from the garden like a grail of light.
They climb out of the mist into a hand
Which holds them till they flower in her sight:

Myrtle for Myrtilus, who died for treachery
And yet found a place among the stars:
The Christmas rose for peace and chastity
– Old stories both, if any of them are.

Yet love remains, although I cannot see it,
The myrtle berries hovering among leaves,
Dark for sorrow, white petals of the rose
Straggling from the gold centre to grieve.

Rapacity and lust will not forbear
And there is no retreat from injury
Except one: *amor vincit omnia*,
And rose and myrtle float in the same sea.

Myrto a woman, Myrtos an island, the Mare
Myrtoum where the rival of Pelops fell.
What light now plays across the sea?
Is there any? O Christmas rose, Noël!

The Birth of Venus

So she stepped naked on the shore and broke
Into a thousand pieces as she awoke
To life in sunlight, and forgot the sea.
The spray blinded all to her symmetry.
Imagination saw a pearly flesh;
The hand that touched it found it cool and fresh,
And moulded it, complete from top to toe.
A liar than asserted that it was so.

The Test

There is no body but the body of
The person who is offered up to love:
Rare body and rare person, for without
Extreme love every person is in doubt.
Where there is none, the scavenger desire
Will still find the material for his fire:
He lacks only the metaphysic twists,
For who can be, if no-one else exists?

Uncertainty

The future is the only thing
That makes for thought, the past is past:
It brought its presents, had its fling,
But what it flung could never last.

The future has not lasted yet
Even the second that it can
And so is good for any bet:
It is the guessing makes the man.

Human uncertainty is all
That makes the human reason strong:
We never know until we fall
That every word we speak is wrong.

Azure may Fade

Azure may fade and then the moon appear
To trick the watcher with her slippery light,
Shadows more real than death steal on the lawn:
The fox peers from the shrubbery, his sharp nose
And bright eyes suddenly extant. O fear!
Dream on, not in myself but in the night.
I feel no trace of it, but when the dawn
Shakes itself, day herself is in the throes.

What must be, will be, and whatever grows
Moves on a pace to death, the moon which hangs
Over the red of east, to nothing goes.
What can the church bell then do but jangle
Its solitary note? – and, as it clangs,
The door is shut before the day begins.
Hope no more: it is the loser wins.

The Sow's Ear

The sow's ear
Is now more valuable than the silk purse,
Nature than art, the silk-worm than the silk.
The breast now swelling with tomorrow's milk
Signifies hope, and the young eyes averse
From any fear.

So the bud too
Promises silently the future flower;
The chrysalis in winter in its sleep
Marks out the place of wings. Nature may keep
Her undertakings in another hour:
So may not you.

The race which came
To Eve by Adam has another plan:
Corrupt the garden and destroy the seed.
Its work is almost done, and former need
Translated into all that pleases man.
The hunted game

Shrinks and the leaf
That once hid Adam's shame dies on the tree.
The rivers die, the seas are empty now.
The fish lie stranded and upon the bough
The fruit is only shadow, and we see
Our time is brief.

The Geese

The turmoil of the geese,
Plodding across the sky with heavy wing
Is in the heart – not theirs, but yours and mine.
We see them pass, and by their flight divine
Our going too: and their diminishing
Tells us our own decrease.

Westward they go,
And where they vanish, there they will be fed.
But we? One tale, if true, would feed us too.
Yet we look backward on the way we grew:
Those who engendered us were left for dead
And we must follow.

Fly with the geese
Who go without the prick of consciousness.
Knowledge is out of place, and speech betrays
The very thought it forms. Then end your days
In the security of nothingness,
And so fly loose.

In Other Words

Words fly like birds across the sky,
And how they go is also why;
There is no other reason.
It is the wind and temperature
Which sends them on their way, for sure,
As suits the changing season.

Words do not come from any mind
Which might belong to humankind,
Or might imagine choices:
They have their sounds and histories,
Adjustable to every breeze,
But they are words, not voices.

The human engine works away,
Begins and lives and ends its day
As best it can, and nothing
That words can add changes its plight,
Nor do they ever change their flight
To give it better ending.

What wonder then if, when we talk,
Although it may affect the chalk
The cheese remains the same?
The words pass by across the sky;
The flesh does not reach up so high,
And so, what's in a name?

So action goes as action must
With noise and pother in the dust,
But oh! our fine pretensions!
Accept no cheques on verbal banks;
Reality returns no thanks
For any man's inventions.

Et in Arcadia ego

And in Arcadia never have I, Charles Sisson,
Passed a day, my days have been otherwise:
I am the old Adam, in another garden,
Driven by tormenting angels from my prize.

The living days are over, and I remember
Only where I have failed, as any might,
On this or that occasion, with him or her,
When almost could perhaps have turned to quite.

So ends a journey which was hardly necessary,
Or so it seems, but what is done is done:
Fact has replaced illusion and I see
With what ineptitude the course was run.

Holà

Words do not hold the thing they say:
Say as you will, the thing escapes
Loose in the air, or in the shapes
Which struggle still before the eyes.
Holà will run upon its way
And never catch up with its prize.

The Trade

The language fades. The noise is more
Than ever it has been before,
But all the words grow pale and thin
For lack of sense has done them in.

What wonder, when it is for pay
Millions are spoken every day?
It is the number, not the sense
That brings the speakers pounds and pence.

The words are stretched across the air
Vast distances from here to there,
Or there to here: it does not matter
So long as there is media chatter.

Turn up the sound and let there be
No talking between you and me:
What passes now for human speech
Must come from somewhere out of reach.

April

Exactly: where the winter was
The spring has come: I see her now
In the fields, and as she goes
The flowers spring, nobody knows how.

The Lack

All is past that is not now:
How long ago it seems!
What was, when life was, is remote
Beyond the reach of dreams.

The life was in the wants we had,
And now what do we need?
Less every day. True riches are
In hope, intent and greed.

How we fared in that starving time
Is less than the starvation
Which gave the future all its worth
And negatived negation.

But now, we only lack the past,
And now is less than then,
Less even than the direst lack
Which will not come again.

Peat

If I could only return to where I am
From where I have been or from the vague reaches
Passing imagination saw, but not I,
The darkness would softly occlude the sky
And all sound faint before the barn-owl's screeches
Or the cry of a solitary lamb.

The sum of everything would be the peat
Which runs cool and dark between my fingers.
It is night itself, a peaceful shower
Which not one minute falls, not for one hour,
But endures while consciousness lingers
And follows it into its final retreat.

Beside the River

Two figures on a river-bank:
A full-grown man, a child of three.
The river passes them, yet stands
For all its flow, as still as they.

River! Exact and noisless time
Passes as you do, and the two
So fixed there now, are not the same
As when your surface caught their eye.

The river holds their gaze, but they
Flow away into emptiness.
Or where? Who knows? Or who can say?
It is not time, but they, who pass.

Figure

It is quite easy to imagine thought
In any animal, as in this sparrow
Hopping reflectively with his mouth full,
Or this blackbird who walks disdainfully,
And at a distance, clearly occupying
A different universe of discourse. We
Have thoughts as well as they, but we have words
To claim more for our thoughts than they deserve.
Men and women have shape and colour, yet
Their thoughts seem verbal custom more than shadows
Of movements they may make or ways they go.
But watch this girl who bends to pick a flower.
Her eyes lighten, blue as what they see;
Her arm stretches, and the fingers flutter;
Her foot arches, the sole presses the ground,
The leg braces, then folds as she kneels;
The thoughtful back and head conclude her purpose.
Thoughts without words: the word is an intruder,
So, when she rises, turns, and shows her flowers,
The whole says, *Look!* and the whole is seen.
Is there another thought beside that one?
Now add a word. O what word can conspire
Against this beauty to make it vanish?
Would not the perfect word corroborate
The whole appearance of the world, and leave
Reality intact of any discourse?
Back to the sparrow and the strutting black-bird,
And you who stand before me in your skin.

Broadmead Brook

O you haunting ghosts, I move towards you.
Could I go over these flooded plains
It would not be to any Paradise:
I came from none and I expect to find none;
It was a long journey, or so it seemed.
The scene changed, and thoughts went through my head,

But even the possibility of knowledge
– Never coveted – seemed no more than a slide
From one thing to another. First the child
Tasting the world, and finding that it hurt;
Then the youth, felled by the bolt of love,
Then labouring where the knowledge was acquired
In self-defence or else in mere ambition.
But late in time and after all deceits,
I came to stand beside Broadmead Brook
As in the very hollow of my hand.
A woman stood there who had been a child
Where in another century my mother
Had played and laboured. Now all was changed,
Yet Broadmead Brook flowed, exquisite woods
Marked her course, for in my fantasy
It was she guarded the bounding deer,
The rabbits and the partridges, and all
Who dare to dream, and be, of England still.

I who am

I who am and you who are
– If we are, as we suppose –
None the less are very far
From knowing what each other knows.

Even the curl of that curled leaf
Is not the same for both our eyes,
Much less a hope, much less a grief,
A memory, or a surmise.

Much less the whole that makes the Is
Of any living creature. I
May utter perfect sentences,
As so may you, who make reply,

But these toy structures are no more
Than any rule held in the hand,
And what your words, or mine, are for
Is not a thing we understand.

So ask the body. It alone
Knows all you know, and it imparts
Little enough of what is known
To what we call our minds and hearts.

So fumbling bodies try to make
Friendship and love as best they can:
None ever was without mistake
And lies by woman and by man.

Man lies by woman, woman lies
By man, and in a common bed.
Where is the rule which truly tries
What is done there by what is said?

On a Drawing

Toi à qui . . . You had never speech;
Only the lines on paper spoke.
No words of mine could ever reach
The silence that you never broke.

Beauty is poised in clear mid-air
And there you are, and there you stay:
For my cold words to find you there,
What silence must they not convey?

The poet and the work of art
Meet where the silence of the word
Encounters lines which have a part
In every echo that is heard.

And you who wore, and were, the flesh
These lines endeavour to translate,
Cannot yourself keep memory fresh
Of what was at that distant date.

It is abstracted lines that live,
While you must die, as others do;
A draughtsman, certainly, can give
A longer memory than you

– But not of you; the temperature
Of flesh, its movement and its thought,
Have no pretence here to endure,
Nor fleeting colour to be caught.

You see the lines the draughtsman drew
Although yourself unmade by time;
I see, and what I see is you
As others saw you in your prime

– Or so your presence is to me,
I boast, I think, I partly lie:
The poem holds you silently
And in that silence words must die.

The Mappemonde

The face, hardly issued from innocence,
Where walls of flesh held fast her feet and hands,
Is fresh as dew, and the emergent limbs,
Tiny at first, grope to achieve their shape.
She has the pulp and surface of a grape:
Do not crush her. It is a new life brims
In that soft skin before she understands,
Or senses congregate and so make sense.

86

Insensibly she grows, but sensibly
Takes in the size and meaning of those blocks
Of hard and soft, those loud and quiet things
Which make the world before the world begins.
Legs and arms do the work of tail and fins,
Propelling this small fish until she flings
Prudence aside, and first kneels, and then rocks
Upon unstable feet for all to see.

So is childhood begun, and consciousness
Grows like a weed within this harmless frame,
Tangled with others as it turns and twists.
You may, indeed, doubt how it can affect
The flesh in which it is rooted, or the aspect
Of that stripped form by which alone exists
All that can have a hope or bear a name.
Yet a face may be thoughtful, none the less.

And thought does not end there. The body flows
Through the slim torso, lengthening arms and legs
– And as they run, dive, frolic and are pleased,
Sayings all quickly seconded by the tongue,
Which speaks also for stomach, heart and lung
And every nerve demanding to be eased.
So every syllable the body begs
Is written in the skin from scalp to toes.

O words joined to the flesh, as once the Word,
And so when shoulders firm and arms grow round
And there is definition in the breasts.
Although the whole frame hesitates to be
The woman who took apples from the tree,
Yet time runs on, the time that never rests,
Until the first maturity is found,
The unmistakable Eve is seen and heard.

Even her smile is ambiguity;
The look and looked-at tumble in her brain
– The arms meant to assist or to entice,
The breasts are apples to the glancing eye,
The patch of hair below writes clearly why.
Yet the whole figure gives more sad advice,

That youth once lost will never come again:
The future comes, in which no one is free.

This was her mother not so long before,
Her mother and her mother, till the past
Runs into darkness. Soon, shaped like a pear,
Her body still resembles theirs, and out
Falls a small girl: the times have turned about,
But she goes, full sail, into different air:
See how her comfortable flesh at last
Rises and falls, breathing at every pore.

Then age. No body is comfortable
In that last scene. No softness of the skin
Can compensate for the receding tide,
Nor any kindness written on the face.
The arms have lost their stretch, the legs their pace.
Yet still only falsity can divide
The outer life from consciousness within,
And at the resurrection all is well.

In the Silence

The silence of my days
Deepens, the wind is still:
Unbroken cloud or haze
Wraps up the world until
The minds which once seemed full
Seem empty, dark and dull.

I speak, and no one hears:
I listen, no one speaks.
There is no sound of tears,
No laughter. No one seeks
The future in the past
Where it must come at last.

And is the future new?
They say so, who ignore
Adam and Eve show through
Today as heretofore.
The murder done by Cain
Is daily done again.

Celebrate if you will
The triumph of your genes:
The past is working still
– That is all that it means.
In every spoken word,
Always, the past is heard.

Perhaps silence is best,
But if there must be speech,
Then watch it closely, lest
It stretches out of reach.
The future is too far;
The past is all we are.

The Rose

What the words carry and the things you say
Must be related, but the saying is you
And what the words carry is history
To which you add your infinitesimal day.
Sweet rose of England, nothing can be true
Except so far as words and you agree.

And how is that possible? My dear,
The tongue you speak must so become your tongue
That it becomes like kisses on your lips,
Given and received at once. Then, without fear,
Your diction answers to the clear line sung
By lutenists, which dips as the voice dips.

So, when words had the colour of the flesh,
And passed from mouth to mouth, and were not laid
Like corpses on a script or on a tape,
The fields rang with laughter, or the fresh
Cry of misfortune. Now speech is a trade,
The word congealed and all meanings escape.

Casualty

It is not the spoken word but the word spoken
In silence, not directed at anyone,
But holding meaning till it spills over,
Which finds its way into the casual mind.
Poetry, ha? The bed-rock of that art
On which those few can build who lose themselves.

Tristia

1

It is because of exile I am here,
The utmost tip of the world, for old age
Brings one to the edge of what one lived among.
Before departure I was of that race
Which passed the time but thought of something else,
But now time fills the whole horizon:
Not what yesterday was or what tomorrow
Will bring, for what it brought is dead,
And what it will, will never come to life.
When will it pass? is all I have to ask.
No-one is implicated in that question
But I who now no longer live among
Even those who see me now as I do them.
But 'as' is not the word I should have used,
For age has given sight in its own blindness,

And no impression is conveyed to me
Which tells me it is here that I belong.
I am the utmost tip of what once was,
Beyond which there is nothing but the sea;
The stationary Pontic cold holds all.
I look towards it, not to those I know,
Though casual bodies hurrying in the street
May hold the eye enough to make a glance,
But where they go is not where I will go:
I turn back to the water and I am lost.

2

No-one will speak to you, nor you to any:
This is the end of all communication
Which was the hope which brought you to this end
And served delusively to coax you on.
The road that leads to death goes single file,
And so it always was. Though each in turn
Surrounds himself with dreams of other minds,
The bodies which should hold them have no voice.
The voice of every lonely traveller
Is loud with silence as the company
He sees around him as he passes on.
Why then these verses? Nothing can be heard.
But speak on as you will, you who are young.
Collude with one another on the way:
Proximity may do what words will not.

3

The hollow name of Love sounds through the streets,
The newsboy crying while the city burns.
The lack of any purpose of my own
Cries louder, and the city is consumed.
The state denies the Church, the Church the state;
The promises of neither have come true,
Or so it seems, here at the door of death.

4

The past is only past which never present was:
Nor is there present now but that vain show of past.
Reality has faded into dream
– A dream without cohesion or event.
Oddities now show nothing but oddities,
For meaning has escaped. Where purpose was
Is nothing but consecutive array
Of matters past which do not matter now.

5

The day is over and the night begins,
But what is day which so resembles night?
Forgetfulness and sleep are of a piece.
The tail-end of the world: and here am I
Pledged to a narrowing prospect. I stand here
While the world fails or falters in my eye.

6

Here on this promontory by the sea,
Speech has no meaning, yet we use it still:
The flagged signal, the gesticulation,
Serve better to elicit a reply.
Yet we walk on, dazed and with hollow voice.
The empty shell you see is what you hear:
The tolling bell will tell the truth at last.

7

The crystal world that was, when I was there:
The broken morning and the silver eve,
The flashing woodland and the dew on grass,
The moon lighting up what the sun has left.
Such a world must be somewhere, but not here.
Even the sea breaking upon the rocks.
Crashes no more, but laps this final shore,
Soon to be frozen. There is wind,
But only hissing as it sidles by.

O send the blustering past in new array,
And let me find the quartz within the stone.

8

The naked person is the only one
Who speaks within the chatter of our speech:
There is no truth in reason or abstraction.
They are the garments that the body wears,
The chatter of the magpie, not the bird
Which walks before the eye in black and white.
The body gives direction to our speech,
As to our thoughts: your shape is what you are,
And what you are is what I seek to know.
The brilliant knowledge which escapes me here,
At this far tip of the world, is what the mind
Can take immediately from what it sees,
Plain without any need for explanation.
So strip before my eyes and speak in tune
With what you are, and that will be the truth
– A momentary revelation
To clear the clouds which else envelop me.
But if you think cloud is where I belong,
Pile on your clothes and chatter in the words
The magpie uses and the world applauds.

9

Speech cannot be betrayed, for speech betrays,
And what we say reveals the men we are.
But, once come to a land where no-one is,
We long for conversation, and a voice
Which answers what we say when we succeed
In saying for a moment that which is.
O careless world, which covers what is there
With what it hopes, or what best cheats and pays,
But speech with others needs another tongue.
For *a* to speak to *b*, and *b* to *a*,
A stream of commonalty must be found,
Rippling at times, at times in even flow,
And yet it turns to Lethe in the end.

10

I am the place where I belong,
For other self or place is not:
The horror of the world extends
Beyond that bourn and never ends.
No friend, no other haunts that space
Which, empty as infinity,
Means no more to me than myself.
Send me particulars and limits,
The tactile and the visible.
Here only nullity is left:
What was lost has lost its place
– No, place has gone as time has gone,
And I have never been, nor am.